Intensive Wind

Charles Schlee

ISBN: 978-81-8253-708-8
First Edition: 2021
Rs. 200/-

Cyberwit.net
HIG 45 Kaushambi Kunj, Kalindipuram
Allahabad - 211011 (U.P.) India
http://www.cyberwit.net
Tel: +(91) 9415091004
E-mail: info@cyberwit.net

Printed at Repro India Limited.

Contents

the name

unsure of what
my name might be
yet knowing i was more
than just an accident of birth
and circumstance
i looked
within the depths of me

i sought a name that said
i'm not afraid
to tread new paths

and since i am one too
i thought
right off
of animals

of horses
and of bears
of cats
and dogs
of squirrels
anteaters
and hares

but
in the end
though some could be companions

i saw none of them
as me

and then
the image of a gray wolf
unexpectedly
emerged

of course
i hadn't just been waiting for
some random bird
to perch upon a limb
or some stray cat or dog
to wander to my door
for in a thing as personal as this
there had to be
a certain kind of fit

and so i went online

i learned
we both are social

when we mate
we mate for life

communication
is important to us both
although i like to think
that mine involves
a lesser incidence
of whines
and howls

and barks
and growls

and we both thrive
in many kinds
of habitats

except when hunted
nearly to extinction

lots of images
passed through my mind
but one
kept coming back

the image
of a gray wolf
standing all alone
and gazing
at a rising sun

i knew
my name was
gray wolf
welcoming the dawn

the autumn gift

it started just before
the sun began to rise

it had been forecast
on the evening news
and so was hardly a surprise

in spite of it
he went outside
to start his walk

it seemed the thing to do
based on his inner talk

and as he walked along
he couldn't help but see
the snowflakes on the ground

except on sidewalks
streets
and such
he saw them all around

he saw a woman
quickly cross the street

she then came toward him
giving them a chance to greet

as he continued
on his way
it seemed the snow had come
to stay

to him
it didn't matter

trudging through the snow
had always seemed
his hiking skills
to flatter

then he thought
he heard a voice

to listen closely
was his choice

for after all
not many people passed him
on his walk

and there was hardly ever anyone
with whom to talk

and as he listened
to the voice
that started as a blur
a second one
began to stir

whence came
this chatty sound

he turned around
and saw two women
he had often seen before
and of whose friendliness
he yearned for more

as they approached
he greeted them

they smiled
and said hello

once they had passed
he reached the fountain
and then turned to go back home

while looking at the lights
along the road
he watched the flakes of snow
that danced before them

and felt grateful
for this unaccustomed
autumn gift

my tridentine mass[1]

i simply want to go there
something in me tells me that i do

i see me start to take a step
in its direction

as i do
i feel a certain youthfulness
and joy

and yet
my soul is sad

i feel like winds are blowing strongly
deep within

but surely i am moving toward my source
the maker of my world

a world in which
i've often erred
in ways that make me feel ashamed
in need of pardon
and of strength

---

[1] This poem was inspired by the Tridentine Mass, the traditional Latin mass of the Roman Catholic Church as standardized at the direction of the Council of Trent (1545-1563) and first issued in 1570.

i feel your presence
you who'll listen
you who'll care
you who'll help me rise
above the burdens that i bear

i open up to you
and ask
that my iniquities be purged
so i
to peace
awaken

feeling now my burdens being lifted
i rejoice
and welcome you
into my heart

i know
that you will light my path
and cleanse my heart and lips
so i can learn the lessons
that await

i ask
that you accept
what i now offer

in the end
of course
it's only me

my flesh
my blood

what more
can anybody give

remembering your suffering
and that of those
who've gone before
i ask you
humbly
and contritely
for the help i need
to wash my hands
and walk in innocence

as you receive
the life that in me flows
i feel your presence radiate
throughout my world
and ask
that you
who are beyond my limitations
offer me
each day
the nourishment i need
to shed my errors
and to clothe myself
in peace

once filled with grace
i too can listen
and can care

i too can help me rise
above the burdens that i bear

i too
despite my errors
in divinity
can share

the leaf

it had budded
and had grown

like many of its peers
it never had left home

symmetrical and green
the handsome little leaf
had felt secure
those many months
when swaying
boldly
in the wind

but then the air got colder
and the little leaf turned red

the day arrived
when it no longer could hold on

and off it fell

it was a graceful falling
as it floated through the air
until it came to rest
upon the ground

its odyssey not done
the little leaf

was quickly greeted
with a gust of wind

obligingly
it pirouetted
till it lost its balance

yet no sooner had it come to rest
once more
upon the ground
than it was jostled
by another gust of wind
that blew it even further
from its home

the leaf
compliant in its poses
finally
lay motionless
upon the ground

was this the journey of a lifetime
for this little leaf

or did its wandering
live only in the memory of
a nearby leaf
that
clinging
saw it go

and wondered
as it sensed its own branch swaying in the wind

and its own reddish hue

if stronger winds were yet to blow

ad altare dei[2]

i was an altar boy
and spoke it
many times

not always sure of what it meant
i liked the sound

it had a special quality
an otherness
that drew me toward it

once in high school
i took latin classes
every term

for me
this language was
much like a flower
opening its petals
to the sun

i'd often lose myself
in its vocabulary
and its rules

---

[1] These words occur in the opening section of the traditional Latin mass of the
Roman Catholic Church: Introibo ad altare Dei = I will go to the altar of God.

the complexities of conjugations
and declensions
stretched my understanding

and the order
in which words occurred
was challenging

i often sat in silence
covering my ears
to help me concentrate

i then went on
to study other languages
from which
it always has been hard for me
to walk away

i guess i've always wanted
introire ad altare dei[3]

as i'm older now
i cannot help but ask
what is the mystery
that draws me to a language

fascination
for a culture
not my own

---

[1] to go to the altar of God

a feeling
that i'm part
of others' lives

a chance to grow
beyond
what i've become

perhaps the reasons
for the mystery
are simply mysteries

regardless of the reasons
languages have always beckoned me

i often hear them whisper
from the corners
and the stairwells
of my mind

and when i listen to their voices
even though
at times
unsure
i feel a strength
so often buried
by the things i'm doing
and the things i've done

the strength
to clothe myself
in otherness

and find myself
once more

of

for him
to be was never
to be next to
or on top of
or before
or even after

no

for him
to be
was to be of

to be a kind of
reaching out

but not the kind that grabs
and pulls

for he would always leave things
where
and as
they were

and yet there was
a kind of
touching
between him

and that
which he was of

he wasn't of for long
of course
for soon
what he was of
was gone

and then
he had to of again

he couldn't live
without that touching
between him
and something
he was of

sometimes
he even tried
to be a gymnast
and be of
what he was of

until
of course
he fell
and then
once more
was merely of

and so he lived
until the day arrived

he could
no longer
of

now there are rumors that
his comrades
at his funeral
had hoped
to say a word or two
about his life

and yet
despite their efforts
and an extra round or two of beer
all they could say
was that

they never really knew
what he was of

the sparrow

walking
in the cool morning air
he
suddenly
was reminiscing

he had worked on it
for many months

his book
that is

to him
it mattered
what he had to say
though others
rarely
looked his way

at times he pictured others
reading it
and asking him their questions
which
of course
he answered
sparking
thus
a lively

private
dialogue

he often thought about his book

and he
of course
like any writer
knew it could be better

so
one day
he started to revise it

then
for many weeks
he struggled with his thoughts

was this the right word
or was that
would this idea help
or that

until
one day
he felt that
finally
he got it right

they surely now would listen

after all
he merely wished

to share with them
new ways
that they could be
new verities
that they could see

and as he walked away
from his meanderings
he saw a sparrow

it just stood there
feet away
and looked

a sturdy cloth

tired from his wandering
he sat
and looked into the distance

then he had the thought
that many times
had left him sweating
his heart pounding in his chest

the purpose
of the human journey
is to weave the threads
of multicolored lives
into a sturdy cloth

now captivated
by this wondrous thought
he asked himself
how it had come to him

what had he done
to be so wondrously possessed

and then he thought about the day
when
sitting all alone
he had the guiding thought
that each of us
must name

the spirit of humanity
that dwells within us

yet the way
that spirit lives in me
is not the way
that spirit lives in you

a way belongs
but to the one
who walks that way

and it is only after
i've named mine
and you've named yours
that each of us will know
the part we've yet to play
to weave the cloth of us

as dusk began to fall
he had the grateful thought
that all of us
can share the nickname
weaver of the cloth

the darkness

finally
the sun came out

a chance
once more
for thoughts to sprout

and yet
though thoughts are hard to see
without the light

and sunny days
may give our thoughts
their might

that doesn't mean
our thoughts
are right

or even
that they're all that bright

yes
basking in the sun
can certainly be fun

and there are times when
with our thoughts
we go on quite a run

but
in the end
the sun shows
only what we've done

the darkness shows
what we have won

the tree

it had lost its leaves
and stood there
naked
in the wind

looking
so it seemed to me
a bit chagrined

its smaller branches swayed
now to the north
now to the south
with little time to rest

its larger branches
with more dignity
thought measured movements
served them best

as for its trunk
though it did little to allure
it seemed in truth
secure

but with a lean
as if to say
things are not
what they seem

yet if you think
it soon will fall

well

we'll just wait and see
who wins this call

# of an evening fair

he didn't really know
that things
would turn out so

how could he then
have fathomed
what he'd one day be

we move along
in hopes our lives
will make a song
not knowing that
the notes will
in the end
go flat

so
as we all
he chased his dreams
at frantic pace
while never looking back
not realizing
how the odds
were always stacked

then came a day
he sensed
he could no longer stay

although his time
now drawing to a close
was missing still the melody
that he had sought
through all those years
he sat
resignedly

not on his usual mat
but in a chair

in witness
of an evening fair

the beating of the drum

the sun was out
the birds were singing
and the air was fresh
and cool

he'd wandered up a hill
when suddenly he heard it

captivated
he just stood
and listened

then he looked around
and saw a young boy
in the distance
beating on a drum

as is the way of life
he had to get back
to his daily chores
so turned
and left his vantage point

once down the hill
though he had much to do
he couldn't help but think
about the boy
off in the distance

and the sound
the drum had made

a herd of wild horses
suddenly ran past
and when he saw their dust
he thought once more
about the boy
and once more heard
the beating of the drum

then he decided to experiment

so he began to think
of chores he'd yet to do
and how he planned to do them
then
he thought once more
about the boy
and once more heard
the beating of the drum

both curious
and kind of stubborn
he performed experiments
for many days

at times he thought just of the boy
at others of the drum
while at yet others
of the movements
of the hands

and every time
he heard the beating of the drum

there came a day
he heard it
with no thoughts of boy
or drum
or hands

he simply heard it

it was thus
he learned a lesson
he would carry with him
all his life

to hear the beating of the drum
he didn't need to see the boy
off in the distance
or the drum
nor did he need to see
the movements of the hands

it was enough
to be a young man
standing on a hill
and listening
to a distant sound

edges

it crawled onto the petal's edge
and paused

until it wanted to explore

perhaps to find
a bite to eat

or a companion

maybe just a different view

and then
the little bug began to crawl
along the edge
as was its custom

fearful of a sudden fall
it held on tightly
as it trekked along

at last
still clinging to the petal's edge
it found a speck to eat
and was content

it rested for a while
then wanted to return
to whence it came

but didn't want to undertake
so long a journey

so it turned
and pulled itself
onto the petal's upper surface

now no longer on the petal's edge
it found that it could crawl
so much more quickly than before

it had a better grip
and didn't have to worry
about balancing along an edge
from which
at any moment
it might fall

and then it stopped

the little bug was back
to where its journey had begun

its joy was overwhelming
as it realized
how quickly it could crawl
by simply not remaining
on an edge

it wasn't even sure
if one should call that
crawling
but decided

it would save that disquisition
for another day

before this sudden metamorphosis
the little bug had looked on edges
as if they were nothing more
than something to be clung to
crawled on
searched for food

but now it viewed an edge
for what it truly was

an edge of something
that was not itself an edge

the little bug had learned
that if it held onto the something else
instead of onto edges
it could move so much more agilely and swiftly
through its world

the lesson[4]

he frowned

she told him *wer*

but dear
he said
i wanted to know where

and so she told him *wo*

that's what
he said
he needed now to know

and on he wrote

he frowned again

she told him *wie*

but dear
he said
i wanted to say me

and so she told him *mir*

---

[1] The words in italics are German: wer = who, wo = where, wie = how, mir = me (dative), fromm = religious, aus = from, wenn = if or conjunctive when, and wann = interrogative when.

that's what
he said
he needed now to hear

and on he wrote

he frowned again

she told him *fromm*

but dear
he said
i wanted to say from

and so she told him *aus*

that's what
he said
he needed to find out

and on he wrote

he frowned again

she told him *wenn*

but dear
he said
i wanted to ask when

and so she told him *wann*

and this goes on
and on

and on

what's that you say

no these aren't lyrics
of a favorite song

but just a poem
that is getting rather long

so i suppose
we'd best be moving on

the glance

it began
with just a look

but not just any look

it was the kind
that leads one
to a book

and led he was

almost invisible
upon the shelf
there sat a smallish book
resignedly
afraid
that he would stray

and yet
it didn't need to fear

you see
for him
its narrow spine
was but a hook
that pierced
and drew him in

as there he stood
his eyes now riveted
upon the book
he knew
he had
to open it

now heading
to the shelf
to reach for it
he nearly shook
and felt his heart
begin to palpitate
his palms
to sweat

yes
there it was
just sitting
on a shelf
in all its regal splendor

if
that is
a simple jacket
royalty
bespeaks

confiding in
the coming
of the day
when someone

finally
would look its way

how long
it must have waited
in its silent nook

to think
a glance
was all it took

the cradle

in his early months
he lived
much like a turtle
in its shell

though his was made of oak and cloth
with playthings dangling
here and there
that he could touch and move

he spent much time in nature
up against a tree
suspended from a branch
or on his mother's back
observing all the colors
and the shapes
and listening
to the novel sounds
around him

sometimes he was visited by birds
exploring a new cooing sound

but mostly he just sat
and watched the drama
that took place around him
and the animals
that never seemed to mind
his movements

or his sounds
and always answered
with their own
as if to say
we too can play

now sitting motionless
now in a gentle breeze
that tossed his cradle to and fro
he would converse
with birds
and dogs
and squirrels
groundhogs too

deeply
in the poetry of life
immersed

the cat's meow

she walked into the hall
and then meowed

we told her to be quiet

she walked into the living room
and then meowed

we told her to be quiet

she walked into the hall again
and then meowed

we told her to be quiet

then we heard her
in her litter box

she finally was quiet

a sacred place

as they drove
around the town
they saw a church
up on a hill

its architecture
and its grounds
intrigued them

so they stopped
and parked
then tried the door

it opened
so they entered

sitting in a pew
just taking in
the statues
and the windows
and the cross
he knew this was
a sacred place

it made him feel
much like the church he'd gone to
in his youth

where he just knew
that from whatever depths
he
to new heights
could soar

it was the kind of place
to which he always
had been drawn

one of the few in which
he felt
that he belonged

he couldn't help but hear
its silent voices
as its sculpted movements
beckoned him

it was a place
he'd not have left
unless he'd needed to

but need
he did

and so they walked back
to their car

yet
as they drove away
he still could hear
its voices

still could see
its movements
beckon him

and wondered
if he had the strength still
to new heights to soar

the figure in the mirror

it's like he knew
right from the start
the life he wanted

though at times
he found it hard to say
he knew
within his heart

he often wondered
what he might have been
if he had been
what he had wanted

and at times he pictured
other paths
than those he'd taken

often longing
for the life
that might have been

at times he felt
like one
just wandering
alone
along a dry and dusty road

like one
unseen
within a crowded room

like one who reaches
for a hand
just as it pulls away

at times
he felt offended

other times
he almost didn't care

and there were times
when tears welled from his eyes

how different was this life
from what he had envisioned
in his youth

from what he had been living for
through all those years

he felt like
he was drowning
in a sea
of emptiness

then
with a movement faint
he noticed

to one side
a mirror

as he looked
he saw a figure
looking back

the more he looked
the more he felt
that he was in the presence
of the friend
who'd always been there by his side
the one
from whom he'd never had to hide

he was transfigured
as he looked
into the eyes
that saw the eyes
that saw the figure
in the mirror
turn
and walk away

the smile of his eyes

he had been ill
for many weeks

we tried force-feeding
but it didn't really help

and when he walked
he listed to the left
and to the right

his eyes were sunken

he was but a shadow
of the cat that
one day
showed up on a windowsill
to stay

he mostly slept
though there were times
we had to waken him
to give him food
or medicine
or water

then he slowly would list back
to where he slept
behind some furniture
where we could hardly reach him

this went on
for several weeks

one day
i petted him
for several minutes
then i stretched out
on the floor
nearby

he slowly walked
to where i lay
climbed on my chest
and
for a while
i felt his fragile presence
moving up and down
in rhythm with my breaths

for him
perhaps this was a chance to cuddle

or a change of pace

it might have even been
goodbye

eventually
he wandered back
to his accustomed spot

a week or so thereafter
hope for a recovery

now gone
we took him
to the vet

adhering to the clinic's covid protocol
we parked and called
they came and picked him up
then let us know when they were ready

knowing that we wanted to be with him
at the end
they met us near a bench
outside the building
where we sat
and petted him

i held him
as he fell asleep
not ever to awaken
or to jump onto my lap
for me to scratch his head
and chin
or hug and kiss him
as he purred
and looked at me
contentedly

we sat until we
numbly
took him to the car
and drove back home

then in the morning
having found a quiet spot
i dug a grave
back toward the fence
and buried him

i marked it
with a rock
though hardly needing a reminder
of a cat
who'll always
have a place
that's safe
and warm
if not within the ground
in which i buried him
at least
within the depths
of me

i used to tell him
as we sat and cuddled
how i wished
we could have been
companions
out in space
discovering the universe
together

it is only now
i've come to realize
the moments
that we spent together

were our real universe
created
by the way we touched
each other's lives

no doubt
i'll often
see his grave

like when
i step onto our deck
or mow the lawn
or wander through my mind
longing for my friend

no doubt
there will be times
when i'll feel sad
remembering the way he looked
in his last days

no doubt
there will be times
i'll tell him that
i'm sorry
that he's gone
that
in the end
all i could do
was sit
and let him drift away

but then i'll look at him
and see
within those dark
and sunken
orbs
the smile of his eyes

and hear him
faintly purr

back to work

i didn't know
what i would write
yet had that anxious
driving
feeling
that i'd had so often
and i knew that it was time

i wandered through the house
and when i reached the sliding door
that opened to the deck
i stopped

as i was looking out the door
i saw a wagon pull into a driveway

though i'd seen the wagon often
it seemed somehow different now

it headed toward a carport
and then backed onto the grass
turned toward a tree
and stopped

puzzled by the point of this odd ritual
i glanced around

then noticed a gray fender
jutting from the carport
nearly hidden by a shed

and as i stood
two cats approached the car
and sat expectantly

a man got out
a string of objects
maybe christmas decorations
dangling from one hand

now up in years
the man walked slowly
toward a house
when
suddenly
a kitten started running playfully
as kittens often do
then
just as quickly
disappeared from view
along with man
and ornaments

the cats that had been sitting by the car
got up
one stretching in its feline way
and headed toward the house

i glimpsed the chickens
near the house
unruffled
as i calmly turned
to get back to my work

looking

his awareness
was astounding
in its breadth
and depth

for all he had to do
was look

and there it was
perhaps again
perhaps not yet to be
perhaps the first time
likely not the last

he liked to look
it was his favorite hobby

if he lacked
a chance to look
what would he do

he surely couldn't
simply sit around
and lack

one day
he took a look at
well
his look

for
after all
there wasn't anything
he couldn't look at
once his mind was set

and as he looked
he was perplexed

he knew
something was lacking

it just had to be

this couldn't be
the way a look
would look

and so he looked around
to see if he could find
the something
lacking from his look

he saw his cat

but when he looked
back at his look
the cat was gone

he saw a piece of cheese
he'd left out of the fridge
now lying shriveled
on a plate

but when he looked
back at his look
the piece of cheese
was nowhere to be found

it was as if the lack
just hung around
and wouldn't leave

so there he sat
just looking at his look

at least
it hadn't gone the way of
cats
and shriveled cheese

and then
as if by chance

for he didn't do it on purpose
after all
all he was really trying to do
was to find out what his look
so stubbornly now lacked

as he sat looking
at his look
and trying hard
to find out what it lacked
he suddenly felt thirsty

heading toward the fridge
to grab another can of beer

he stubbed his toe
against a shoebox
he had tossed
onto the floor
the day before

now looking at himself
bent over
grabbing for his foot
he felt a twinge of pain

and chuckled
as he looked

for suddenly
he knew
it wasn't just a look

it was a painful look

and then he realized
he almost always
fondly looked at cats

though usually he looked
a bit disgustedly
at shriveled cheese

excited at his new discovery
he couldn't help but think
about the ways he looked
at other things

at tv shows
he really liked
he looked enjoyably

while at his wife
at times
he looked desirously

though at his next door neighbor
not so much

this was
for him
quite a discovery

and he was grateful

for he'd likely not have guessed
a look was never
just a look
but was a way of looking too
had he not stubbed his toe
while thinking about
what a look
so stubbornly had lacked

though he was curious
about the ways he looked
at many other things
and people too

just looking at his looks
was growing tiresome

and so
when drinking beer
popped once again
into his head

he looked away

the crack

i saw it
winding to the left
and to the right
showing off
its subtle kind of might

i couldn't really tell
where it was going
for it seemed
a special kind of indiscretion
to be showing

as if it
could simply change its mind
at any place
or time

and then
a beetle scurried on its way

apparently
it didn't have all day

i wonder what
that beetle would have done
if it had reached the crack

would it have tried
to cross

or maybe it
such courage
would have lacked

i don't suppose
i'll ever know
the beetle quickly choosing
far into the grass to go

as i walked on
i glanced down at the crack
now fading from my view

i didn't feel remorse for leaving
after all
it was my walk
and i
to keep on track
had little time for sidewalk cracks

what's more
i knew
it didn't need a chaperone

for clearly
it could snake along its chosen path
quite on its own

into the wind

we each must choose a name
it tells us how the wind
blows through our frame
and how it plants the seedlings
of our passing fame

the day
i couldn't stop imagining
a gray wolf
standing on a mound of dirt
or rock
and watching as the sun began to rise
i knew
somehow
what i was looking at
was me
and how i
at my deepest depths
must be

regardless of the days
that have
or will have
gone
i always will be
gray wolf
welcoming the dawn

it's how the spirit of humanity
flows through me
tweaking every movement
that i make
and every breath
however slow or fast
i take

we each must give ourselves a name
it is our only lasting fame

the way we say that
this is me
that this is how
i choose to be

now some will do it casually
while others
prone to rituals
will do it in a ceremony

though our ways may differ
how we do it
matters not

for each of us
a name has got

the name that
one day
tossed about
we reached into the wind
and caught